Drown these Butterflies in Whisky

Drown these Butterflies in Whisky

By Toby Darling

WALNUT STREET
— PUBLISHING —

No butterflies were harmed in the making of this book. Words, photography, and cover by Toby Darling.

ISBN: 978-1-967230-06-8

Walnut Street Publishing
1673 South Holtzclaw Studio 14
Chattanooga, TN 37404
www.walnutstreetpublishing.com

For whom these words are written.

I will write for you
Far longer past the ink dries
Or paper blackened
Wells of ink spilled in the sun
I will write in blistered ink

Cheers
pt. 1

Sriracha

The heat of life
it's been too strife
And swift in it's shortcomings

This karmic dream
of love unseen
In search of one's Prince Charming

And with its spite a
taste of spice
Has been so quite alarming

Coffee

I'll stand waiting in line for eternity
To fix my lips on your warmth
To feel the sensation of jubilance
though falsely given, as if a drug

The subtly in which you steam,
I hastily move forward in dismay
You've burned the effort
and left a bad taste in my mouth

Thursday Night

Thursday night. Red wine. Full glass. She's with her friends, but she isn't present. She's staring at her drink - occasionally swirling it. Her friends are talking among themselves and with a few guys who approached them earlier. She's sitting to the side, legs crossed, red dress, and black bangs. All of her friends are blonde.

His Order:

Water, less ice, no lemon, straw
Twice-cooked pork - extra spicy
Side steam rice
Hot and sour soup in the winter
No fortune cookie

Burning

"I feel like your fire is burning out."

Said the bartender, after seeing me out
for the first time in a few months.

"How did you know?"

Toast

I've drunk enough to know the answer
isn't at the bottom of a glass
Or the liquid held inside.
It's the hands
behind the grains
behind the grapes.
The hands
on the glass
Cheering one another
Reaching closer.
The hands holding
each other
Around the back
Around the head
The lips on the glass
Whispering love
Affections
Sipping
Drinking each other in
smiling
laughing
crying
Celebrating today
Forgetting yesterday
Ignoring tomorrow.

Clementine

Oh, my darling,
I do find you tantalizing
For the juice of the clementine
Holds no structure to the nursery rhyme
Sweet, fair, and supple citrus
You would be my only wish...
...if I were granted three wishes.

Champagne

Toast to the night
To kings, to jesters
We raise our glasses
To show good gestures
Of will and flight and
To hide our sorrows
Drink... for there may be
No tomorrow.

Gray Skies & Wet Asphalt
pt. 2

Fall

Today I noticed it was fall.
Crisp air carried by gentle breezes
Leaves carried with and land far
Faded green to gold and crimson
Streets covered by remnants of what was.

Today I noticed it was fall.
A season gone and replaced anew
Of shorter days and longer moons
An extra layer, a scarf, a sweater
Another reminder that I fell for you

Behind the Clouds

I struggled to see behind my cold breath
And I could feel the thin air in my chest,
But thoughts of you were warmth to save from death.
These grey skies have clouded me in the west
And have painted an endless horizon,
Yet in the haze I saw the sun suppressed.
I stood there and I felt my skin tighten
And gazed at what seemed like a stretching void,
Then closed my eyes so you might let light in.
The last of these winter winds now deployed
And the spring remains to be uncertain.
And though there is much more we can't avoid,
I know that clouds can turn into mountains.

Incomplete

I reached into the air outside the glass
And felt my hands get cold against the wind
And cooled my mind to something new
My heart became warmer than before
I brought those hands back in
Fresh and new I curled my arms to my chest
And felt my heart shutter against the skin
My heart became warmer than before
And as I began to balance out
I felt the urge to do it again
To experience that rushing urge
Of a feeling that could make me feel warm again
And so I reached back out
Hoping to bring you back in.

Leave

My breath; seen in autumn air.
Exhales expressing in a silent hymn
Are choreographed as the season leaves.
Exposed by axis rotation and cold.
Always now, I tell too much truth then fall
Into sleepless slumbers throughout the night...

Must your smile shine at night?
Must your breath be what my lungs crave as air?
Must I, again, infatuate and fall
For a woman who sings another hymn?
'suppose I've grown accustomed to the cold.
My heart speaks: Eyes to tears, as branch to leaves.

Better this way, lest she leaves.
And hours gained throughout an endless night.
And quilts, coats, and fire can fight the cold.
And what better breaths than unbridled air?
I digress, because I'll lose to her hymn,
For when I see her, again I will fall.

...now is when I always fall
Victim to my own words which yells and leaves
My mouth, singing a sentimental hymn,
That will only reach at the depth of night.
My throat swells and chokes these words into air,
Forced to share these lines that will leave me cold.

No. I'd share despite the cold.
For this is love and not just a mere fall.
And these feelings are not a change in air.
They lay strong. Yes! Stable and not what leaves.
With a heart that burns bright against the night.
And three hundred sixty nine breaths a hymn.

And yes! These sounds are my hymn!
No matter if it hot or if it cold.
I will sing in the day or in the night.
And will carry these words until I fall.
or... at least in hope that it never leaves.
That these songs are songs, and not only air.

Of course this hymn suffers fall,
And the cold parallels these autumn leaves.
But for just one night, I'd sacrifice air.

A pond below swells,
And carries loves last further
Down streams and rivers.
Bless your flowing waterfalls,
Which will fill my open wounds.

Snowflake

The fair snowflake contrast against the velvet sky
As it falls in crisp breezes and tumbles through the night
Swaying within tall trees between the boney branches
Yet this unique flake falls gallantly, as if she dances

Little Green Leaf

There was a little leaf who was so green
Who would blow in the wind to dance and laugh
Days when the sky would rain and lose its gleam
The little leaf would drink to gain strength back
She gazed towards the light to feel alive
To then fall asleep when the sun would dip
But then the air will feel so cold and dry
And all the other leaves will turn to crisp
For she was evergreen throughout all the year
And the autumn leaves would fall to attest
That when come white blankets drape oh so near
She realized all her friends had laid to rest
But soon the sun would spring so bright its light
And our little green leaf will feel alright

Springs First Flower

Below these empty trees of the cold's past
Lay fields of white snow so pure and gallant.
Through the bare limbs above the sun may cast
To soften the ground to make vibrant.
Oh, these eager trees will remain patient,
So spring may warm the brittle winter air.
The snow may drip, but shall not be vacant!
For the spring's first flower will blossom there.
Then the trees leaf out to shade and to care
The snowdrops reach above in jubilance,
And fill the barren land in supple fair
To flow and sway in dancelike unison.
Yet, without the cold none of this could be
What the winter gave and the spring set free.

Storm

I watched the rain last night
Watching as it performed
I thought, 'How brave the rain,
To jump from clouds roaring.'
Falling to dance insight
To splash in whole reform
I thought, 'How kind the clouds,
To spark night with lightning.'
Crashing into mountains
To light up the dark sky
I thought, 'How can I join,
To splash around dancing?
　　How might I take that flight?'
　　Then thought, 'You are my storm.'

I'll Always Love the Rain

These chilling days of life so uncertain
As we're forced to maintain on solid ground
On days when clocks tick with no progression
Safety and home are no longer around

So, I dream of days when my dreams were hope
And when my breath wasn't stifled by words
Not hidden behind masks and no need to cope
With just a long shot that I might be hers

But I fucked it up by saying too much
And by attempting to whisk you away
Instead, I pushed you much further from touch
And I'm left with dark clouds and skies so gray.

Now, I don't mind the storm for what it's worth.
As I love the rain that dances to earth.

River Blue

River blue eyes for you
Rushing forward to do
Dark lips of tonight, pushed
to tomorrow to gain.

A stare into your gaze
A stop of my knees felled
A breath of yours and mine
I could never abstain.

Speak with lips and dissect
Unspoken to others
A mind to preserve all
And not again do feign

I'll sit still in this sway
And breathe a word of you.

I am just a stone
Still, in your rushing river
Curve my shape and form
Swell your body over me
Cover me in white water

Prevailing Winds

I watch the sunrise
While you sleep in the past
To draw days a bit sooner
And feel nearer to you

I stand in prevailing winds
That swept Appalachia
And over the ocean
That carries your breath to mine

I look up at the moon
when the sun is with you
And see the cast of the earth
Containing the shadow of us

I sleep near the western wall
At the edge of the bed
Though a thousand miles away
To lay closer to you

And I rest in the Irish mountains
That once shared the same range
Before the passage of time
And I keep loving you

Your Eyes

I've built this dock stretched over an ocean
A desert of undrinkable water
No maps or tools, just patience and emotion
But the sun sets and the skies grow darker
Rumbling clouds appear and the waves alter
And lightning crashes like a photo still
Frame by frame these planks begin to tatter
And now I drift on waves of roaring hills
But I am more scared of a creek or rill
Or standing at the shore on solid ground
So far from the clouds and fresh rain to swill
Just leave me floating; I would rather drown
To tell stories of when the clouds withdrew
To see the pale moonlight and ocean blue.

Lily of the Valley

These valley blooms of May
Drape high in early spring
Reaching for the sunlight
To dry its lady's tears

To soon harvest bouquets
With words too hard to sing
I left these bells of mine
In hope they'll reappear

Due in eyes of winter
Reflect on what is lost
Sow the seeds patiently
Blossom within the year

White flowers borne in spray
Behold what beauties bring

Tree of Life

They say, once every three thousand years
A peach rests on the edge of a branch
Thought to give one immortality
And I would share every life with you

Some speak of a fraught tree of wishes
Granted by chanting and offerings
That's gold with mesmerizing aura
So, my every wish would be of you

Others believe in golden apples
Gifted only by Gaia herself
To be delivered to the fairest
Which could be no other, only you

By many, this tree is life itself
Encompassing all nine realms beyond
A source for all that's built on gallows
That contains my every thought of you

By Taos or Hindus; Or Greeks or Norse
A Tree of Life — is a life with you.

Why I Love the Moon

I waxed for the sight of a crescent moon;
Like the light smile of a bright idea.
Yet, this moment falls quick and much too soon,
And light floods the depths of dark maria.
Fold back over to this shared arena,
Then wrestle against this opened gibbous
And broken sanity at full luna.
Soon this too will fleet and dark resurface.
For it's in the night I found its purpose:
What you cannot see is the moon's secret
Those bright highlands are just a blank canvas
And the shadow is the painted credit
Because in this dark is the earth sheltered
Containing you, me, and us together.

———————

The warmth of your laugh
The sweet structure of your lips
In the wind, I blow
As a leaf, weak to your hand
You have brought me to my knee

Forget-Me-Not

Not shy in shade
In love in sun
Midsummer sow
For next year's plot

In winter falls
New seeds undone
In seasons four
If still a thought

So quick succumbed
By way of time
These flowers bloomed
And we were caught

If I must fade
Forget me not

Dark Sea

Why can I not forget all ships that pass?
As memories and dreams of long ago
Be it yesterday or my tomorrow
The breached ocean below the sun casting.
Where is the moon to rip and close my thoughts?
Waves against the earth crashing on the shore
Remnants of the past left among the mor.
Nestled deep and further past measured knots.
And lay rest to my aching affection.
Because I still love what I had forefront
And nothing is gone in this open sea
But I can't explain this recollection
Nor do I care to have all this affront
May the depths of darkness forget for me

Skip

I've not cried in a while
Nor my heart skipped a beat
A longing wish of you
In curtains drawn long past

I saw the stone laid clear
Torn heart and false smile
My ears rang in deaf tones
Of old questions longed asked

An accustomed lifestyle
Memories of a kiss
That won't reconcile
But a shared moment true

I loved you all worthwhile
And will so through and through

Vagabond
pt. 3

Lake Crescent

Mountain mist lay still on the lake below,
as if Olympus' gates spilled onto Earth
to create our heaven; a gift bestowed

And show our timid secrets and our worth.
In a valley lit and shadows dispersed.
A looming mystery, a virgin birth.

Oh, the Old gods have cascaded this pursed
Crescent Lake that holds the deepest fountains.
This serene body clouded by a curse

Now lifted by my eyes beneath mountains.
No rain, or snow, or sleet, or fog can shroud
Us in this range of rigged horizons.

Lay still, North Wind, this love has been avowed.

Tlaquepaque

These cobbled streets are all to mend my soles.
Broken, torn, and weathered stones are where I walk
Trudging along, powered by steam and coal.
If the path behind could find words to talk
or if the road ahead could bear a sign,
I wouldn't need to look above to gawk
Reaching for an umbrella as a line
to lift me up and off this tarnished mass
And live in the heavens with you as mine.
But the sky will remain as fragile glass,
Scattered, stained, with fragments turned into sand.
As I wait for this road to find ends pass,
I will dream of a place above clay land.

Atotonilco el Alto

Granted I was on a trip that was all inclusively provided by Patron Tequila. Granted I was staying at their Hacienda whose housing is built like a luxury hotel, a room at any normal rate would cost more than my month's rent for one night. These gorgeous buildings developed in the early 2000s resting on acres of a well-maintained landscape. All these beautiful things are stuck in the middle of the highlands of Jalisco, further embellished by the geographical scenery which surrounds the valley tucked Hacienda.

All these things... couldn't hide the way of life in the neighboring town less than a mile away. Nor could hide all the dilapidated buildings that seem to house dozens of people. Felled walls of brick lay rest near a newly make-shift pallet wall draped by a thin tarp. Roofs are patched simply by laying down a tarp or putting a pile of debris over the hole. Homes you could easily see into as you're driving by because the building doesn't have a front door. All these destroyed canisters that are now serving as shelters stretched far and wide on tattered roads from the airport to where I sit typing this.

Yet, the people are happy. They look happy. They seem happy. They seem humble, grateful, and loving.

And they were. They were amazing.

Seasons spent barren
In the sky island mountains.
Dense lilies flourish.
Matured. Harvested. And pressed.
To capture your heart's essence

Scotland

Glasgow

A dirty metropolitan. The smell of foul piss looming from alleys contrasted against street art on every corner and back wall. Local teenagers idly stand around historical buildings and monuments with skateboards and speakers. Litter bins overflowing. A certain speedy pace by passing strangers with brightly lit shops behind them. This place is familiar. As if it were copied and pasted in the US. Grungy, youthful, tattered -- punched in the face too much but refusing to stay down. Art. This place is art. Creating and blossoming from cracked sidewalks. A kinetic engineered structure of a city.

Inveray

White stucco buildings float on the loch as we drive in. A welcoming single-laned arched bridge capitalizing a living postcard of a town. Or village? Or hamlet? Who's to say? Friendly people living and working and breathing the town alive. Locals. Callan. Connie. A southern charm of welcoming and charisma, but northern? But southern? A sip of scotches. Dust against the bottle. And tales of escape and imprisonment. Rainy days turn to sunshine and rain again. You just might find a rainbow. And with that luck, fate might bring you back.

Isle of Skye

Tucked in the hills so far away, you're lucky to know you're not alone. Winding roads off cliffs led to the question; are we here on purpose? At the end of the road of dark winds and water, you'll find a cozy couch to rest your weary head. A hearthstone to come back to, and other travelers to share and wonder. Come morning grey the urge of enchantment and majesty hail us out of bed. You'll drive windy single- lane roads as friendly passersby let you through. Pothole after pothole and curve after curve, you'll reach the top of a blind summit and see something you've never seen before. And while the journey to the end is always worth it, it's these destinations that will leave you wordless.

Oban

A worker's inn. A home away from home. A home with new family and strangers you only see on holidays. The cool brother. The racist uncle. The funny sister-in-law. The drunk cousin. A place you might end up resenting. But that you wouldn't regret any of. The cool sea air will blow your hat off if you're not too careful, but a kind hand might help you chase after it.

Wick

As the embrace of the highland mountains flattens out, just past Loch Ness and the city of Inverness, is a land of pastures, hills, and cliffs. Moving forward North lends itself to an idea of escaping reality as you inch closer and closer to the top of the world. Riding a narrow road along the coastline, with small town after small town appearing after a sudden bend or rich castle. You might find yourself graced by farm life inquisitively staring back at you as if they know you're not a "local". Then by the end, you'll find yourself a bench near a cliffside beaten by the North Sea. And you'll look out into the horizon where the clouds and ocean morph together; to see the stars piercing through the night. At this time, you might think to yourself, "Why would I ever go back south?"

Inverness

A city of the highlands, but not a building taller than a mountain. A church might compete. But I don't think the locals care. A place where caring for your neighbor means just as much to a stranger. So much angst and history. The coffee is good. The books are good. You'll have a story to tell by the end.

Edinburgh

Let's find a reason to stay. Dim-lit streets hide the nooks and crannies needed to explore. A looming presence watches and cares for you. A guiding hand for those in the dark. Stone buildings and roads. Colorful characters welcome you and offer you food and shelter. Tinkers will show you the workshop. Old and young come together in a city filled with so much history and lore to push the limits forward and create a home to be proud of. If I didn't have to, I would never leave.

Tomorrow

She stands barefoot on dry and cracked asphalt roads.
"A vagabond," she dreams,
But for now, only her mind attests.
Her love is love,
If love is sincere.

Today

Weathered and torn of life's hardest spites
Dripped beads of tears in the seams
Not a day... she isn't thankful
Here she cares not to impress
Yet, stands tall, vibrant, and smiling for the next.

New Orleans

The French Quarter is all the rager you think it's going to be. Swamped streets of drunken tourists. Plastic cups and beads are littered on every curbside. And the energy of centuries of debauchery in the air. New Orleans is not for the faint of heart.

Grab yourself any frozen concoction you want from just about a hundred of the same colorful bars. Go see music on Bourbon Street, whether buskers on the street or the shitty DJ in a club. Climb up to the second rail and scream at the people below. OR. Venture away by a mere few blocks to any other adjacent street and enjoy the energy of a simple no-frills bar, or craft cocktail lounge so small you wouldn't even be able to park a car in the space. Walk down Royal Street and grab a bite to eat from a cash-only bodega. Get the catfish po' boy.

Wander from district to district aimlessly and what feels endless. Walk with confidence and purpose, because it's surprising how friendly the people are everywhere you go. Most everyone told me not to go more than a few blocks away from the French Quarter, but when I did, I saw more of what the city really is, versus how it's shown to people.

I wish I could offer the best restaurant I ate at during this trip, but funnily enough, the best food I've gotten was a fried oyster po' boy from a cash-only bodega; a fried catfish po' boy from a gas station; and a grilled shrimp po' boy from another corner store. I ate plenty of other food, ate at a nice place with an excellent seafood dish. Had crawfish étouffée from a dinky little spot. An andouille sausage from a guy grilling on the sidewalk. Oh, and a seafood ravioli that was to die for. There was no one spot. I'm happy reflecting back on my choice of purchases. Without question, New Orleans is a drinking town. And while there is plenty of room for that -- I don't think that is the sole defining characteristic of New Orleans. It's the food, the music, and the people.

Metro MTA

We stood aimlessly on the platform waiting
For a car to brighten the dark track we stared long into.
Is it ours? We thought.
Wait... which one is ours?
We had only a moment to resolve.
Didn't matter,
any direction is a direction of exploration
Of adventure and memories to be had.
So we gallivant in these dark and deep tunnels.
Miles and miles of metal to decide
What our next stop could be.
With you by my side,
I'll ride this train local
And love every moment.

Reflection
pt. 4

A Fool

A fool perhaps, that stares into the sun
Blindly disguising foresight intention
To swim in melted wax with retention
And walk in desert sand too soft to run
And fight in battle where no winner's won
Only gruesome pain and blood reception
To drown in sorrow own self infliction
And March and March to the beats final drum
Then yes. A fool indeed... the one that loves
A fool... who fought more than the gods allowed
A fool... who dreamt more than the stars suspend
A fool? No. A man, as pigeons to doves
A man who sees heavens and not just clouds
A man who smiles at the bitter end.

A Kiss

My eyes speak words that my tongue cannot say
   As I listen to yours in the silence
My breath feels faster and my lungs are weighed
   As I'm whelmed by your being and presence
My heart tightens and pounds inside its cage
   As it fills your gaps in ways to mirror
My hands drift behind your waist and your nape
   As I dare pull you closer than ever
My head tilts left and worlds disappear
   As I lean to meet you for the first time
My mouth touches yours and we both whisper
   As the warmth fills our bodies and our minds
Our lips Hold on despite this fleeting start
   As if we were not meant to be apart.

Candlelight

Hot air stifled in a windless chamber
Reluctant pressure has kept my flames drawn.
Fixed atop of wax with a wick that's gone
With an endless fight that I might claim her
Or until my last flickers remainder
Within shadows of my heart as a pawn.
To live in dark until the breach of dawn.
Or rest eternal in a deep slumber.

Remove the dome that entraps my fire
And let my light no longer be hidden
Burn with passion and burn against the blight
And carry forth my heart's deep desire;
A cherub's arrow, a letter given
Signed and sealed with red wax and candlelight.

Depression

My alarm goes off at 9:30 am. I roll over to shut it off. I regret the decision I drunkenly made at 2:00 am to wake up early in an attempt to do laundry. I fall back asleep. 10:00 am. My alarm is going off... "Ughhh..." I think to myself. I forgot I set five alarms on every half hour. I turn them all off. I blink — it's now 2:00 pm, and I honestly have no idea how. I open my laptop and turn on Hulu to play Bob's Burgers; it's a mechanism I use to fill in the loud void of silence. I go start the coffee maker, then hop in the shower.

Suddenly it's 7:00 pm. "How...?" I mutter to myself while lying on my couch still watching, but not watching, Bob's Burgers. There's an empty plate covered in pizza grease on the coffee table, and I realize I still haven't done laundry. I text my friends, "What's everyone doing tonight?" As I wait for a response I start getting dressed because I refuse to waste my day in my underwear. I get in my car, and then my friends respond saying they can't come out because they have work in the morning. I forgot it was Sunday.

I still go out. I drive to my favorite bar. I'm a regular there, so the bartenders know me. They feel like my friends. I call them my friends. I sit alone at the bar scrolling through my phone and not talking to anyone. I pay out after two beers and go home. I put on Bob's Burgers while lying in bed and drink too much whisky. I set a few alarms, then fall asleep.

Do Good

I used to keep this card in my wallet. It was a business card that belonged to a woman I met at a bar a few years ago. She was only in town until morning. She was part of a theatre group on tour and just finished their last show that evening. Her cast mates went to the hotel. She stayed out.

We talked for a couple of hours. Bonded over puns, music, movies, and whiskey. She gave me her card. Told me that if I were ever in New York to hit her up. I'm sure she gave it out of kindness more so than seriousness to that offer.

I never texted her. Never called. Never looked her up. But I held on to that card. I kept it in my wallet for a long time. It was a reminder. A reminder that even at 2 am on a very very early Wednesday morning, I could still meet someone. Have a genuine connection with someone. Have a memorable moment with someone. That there are people out there.

I was searching for the answer at the bottom of a glass. Then I met her.

Drown these Butterflies in Whisky

My forearms tighten whenever she's near
Longing to feel her skin pressed against mine
To speak to her without words or fear
And discover secrets we both might find
My heart beats different, trying to define
Which one of us two is its true owner
As it tries to synchronize and align
Trying to escape just to get closer
My stomach crawling with caterpillars
Has now exploded to house butterflies
Fluttering in attempt to be near her
Wondering if freedom might catalyze
 My mind knows better than wishful thinking
 So I'll drown these butterflies in whisky

Existence

So, I know what existence is to me
Quiet days of solace in gratitude
Mouths of uncompromised self-decisions
And only one alarm in the morning

Though, one thing in the afternoon with you
I have thought of what existence could be
Challenges of encouraged adventures
Both of us scared, trembling, and learning

And, fearlessly filled with much more to see
A day of all of what life can offer
Lofty dreams of an existence of we
To revel in our own dispositions

Yet, existence by my own fallacy
Quiet challenges of revelations.

Ghost

The ghastly ghost that haunts at night
only does so in fear of light.
For the warmth of the sun
reminds too much
of the warmth of life,
of love,
of touch.

When the Morning Comes

We lay holding each other. Only a dim gray light that has breached the windows from the street post outside fills the room. Details of her face are clear even in the darkness. A small scar above her right eyebrow holds my curiosity. The slight curl of her stretching eyelashes. Freckles that are known only to those who have been lucky enough to share the intimate space I'm in now. She turns to look at me, then smiles. A bashful laugh emits. She closes her eyes and turns away.

Her room is small. Her pillows are used. The blanket is soft. Felled shoes rest outside of her open closet door. Our clothes piled in the corner. This is her world when she no longer allows the world to be her host, and I am her guest.

Words are exchanged but seem almost unnecessary. Smiles of wonder and passion are shared through a unique language of which only our bodies can speak. I'll learn more this way.

She's not mine, I'm not hers, because in this moment these possessions don't matter. We belong to no one, yet choose to share the evening together. The future is not a thought. The past does not exist. The present is what we have, and all we have.

Tomorrows are for when the morning comes.

Fifth Word

Empathy is not love forged
It's innate and always true
Born with us and found within
So sealed by a mother's kiss
Yet, no love true than friendship
Picked by us, not Gods thereof
Unless compared to Venus
And the primal urge for bliss
Not from any, but from one
Left to knees to yearn above
Without condition or skew
I yell to heavens with this;
The Greeks have four words for love
I offer one word more — You

Hellfire

You and I know life has not been easy
Our lives burn like fire in the kitchen
For warmth, affection, or a guarantee
That we struggle, ourselves, to find within

But our love runs deeper than black midnight
And the Devil's number screams in terror.
Because what's true, is we will always fight.
For ourselves and life and all that's rarer

Distill our dreams into finer Whiskey
But first, ferment our lofty desire
Complete by age, our maturation key
So warm our souls by Hell's hottest fire

And let us live throughout eternity

Or as long as we want this dream to be.

Olive Branch

What do we make of our own destiny?
In a land of Lords, Kings, and Queens, my Grace.
Bounded by our name and pedigree
We must break the chains and the wheel in place.
A foolish and endless fight for such virtue
But no more foolish than a fight for king
I'll stay a fool for the right to kiss you
And live chivalric in all that it brings
Watch. So that our summer may never end.
That our days are one, is my desire.
In the Seven Seas, the sun can't descend
On our story and song of ice and fire.
    And like Aeneas on the stern his stand.
    I hope to hold an Olive branch in my hand.

I Might Remember

I

This world empty and bare
by superficial green life
I stand as a vessel of nothing
only to trot and dance
Sing the solemn song
and be grateful to earn my
own life back

Might we greet death with
anticipation of
welcomed open arms
of self-callous action

Or might I walk
willingly
into Styx
and hear my voice
to yell for relief

II

It's cold. It's always
cold and dark.
Of us left
we trudge through, forward
I amongst others of
myself

Hollow men, biding breath
moving forward in unison
rhythm of March
yet no fight, but
an urge to suffer

III

Cut our eyes
and let us blister
let us blister
let us blister
cut our eyes to
let us know
this darkness is no longer
our choice

IV

It's a forgiving dream
that tempts us all
but to bite
is to regret

V

Kill me, so I might remember
Kill me, so I might remember
Kill me, so I might remember
In darkness, there is light

Sculpture

My fingers trace the outline of your skin
In darkness, I can see you.
I could sculpt your likeliness in marble
From memory, with eyes closed.

I feel your presence on empty pale nights
Your warmth masks the coldness so
You illuminate the pale moonlit sky
At dusk, I can find the sun

I breathe in your essence from billows left
You enthrall the man within
Awakened by your impression beside
I see you, I come alive

A longful heart that bleeds for none alike
A heart that's yours to hold
To beat in sync with your heart and spirit
I will always shout your name

When I Die

When I die
I want to be cremated
Not because it's cheap or easy
but because I want to be gone

But I want to be present in this world
Divide my ashes among friends
And let my friends scatter a piece of me
somewhere that mattered

Let me live in the soil
in the wind
under the sun and moon
or wade in the water

Let my friends pick
Divide me into pieces
and share me
within your memories

Blood & Crimson

Inevitable crimson.
That streams through my veins and into my heart.
It beats for you alone and no one else.
Cut me open to let this love pour out,
And stare while I tremble on the ground.
How can I speak when I write all my words?

These empty desirous words.
Complemented by my face made crimson.
Scratching your name with my nails on the ground
In an effort to claw you from my heart.
The point is moot; I never want you out.
It's just… without you, there isn't much else.

An inconceivable else.
Fight back with any of these written words.
They have all been made for you to find out.
Hoping that you share this thread of crimson,
And that we are linked by a string and heart.
So that we might soon stand on steady ground.

Oh, this precarious ground.
Swayed and tethered by these thoughts of who else...
Shaking from the pumps of my skipping heart.
Quaking by the weight of these two-faced words.
Fill a fountain with wishes and crimson,
So I might write until red ink runs out.

Please rip this fallacy out.
For I am delusional to your ground.
And I cannot trust my own minds crimson,
Because you are in love with someone else.
And your story carries another's words.
So I'll just sit here with my longing heart.

This irresponsible heart.
That hopes one day you will figure me out.
And that your next chapter might be my words.
That we might walk together on shared ground.
Belief in each other and no one else.
And bathe in oceans as deep as crimson.

But my heart is laid to ground.
I'll not speak out if you're with someone else.
So I'll write these words in blood and crimson.

Focus

How many nights can I go without sleep?
Tossing and turning until the day breaks
With thoughts of you keeping me awake.
Why are these fantasies strong, yet so fleet?

How many days can I go and not speak?
Hesitant of what my truth might forsake.
Accustomed to this suffering and ache.
But can my heart take another skipped beat?

I am frightened that if these feelings stay
That the damage done cannot be reprieved
Trapped inside unrequited fallacy.
So I beg of you, to my own dismay,
To go! Before I become too naïve.
A hopeful wish is not reality.

Drunk

A secret shared by a crooked entrance
too embarrassing to be told sober
but weren't for whiskey, there is no difference
I would speak so that the Gods remember

But to that credit, I would dismember
That I would not be so strong in the day
For it's not about one's own endeavor
But what one may feel on clearest day.

And I will rise despite my heart's dismay
to fight those who try extinguish fire
To shout to all Almighties to convey
that my heart just wants what it desires

Not when if impaired or if in question
You will always be my one confession

Lighthouse

To wade in ocean blue by rivers rush
Against the current of these storming seas
She's the light by coast above waves that crush
Onto brittle rocks felled by raging breeze

A guide to restful shores of newfound land
But bound by nature and of yesterday
She's the grace of promise and I her hand
To live and lust in bounty of bouquets

She's the beauty by which the gods will kneel
And the heart to care for all those around
To dock at the bay and to sudden steal
I'll yell her praise until she's filled with sound

To tell her she's the light in hidden sun
And to speak her name in admiration

Red

Oh, what words to speak when lost in fantasy?
Of her supple lips, and of her blushing cheeks.
I grow tired of this quiet truancy.

My voice lost like rust on forgotten antiques.
These unspoken desires riddle my bones,
And my heart has only just learned to beat.

Will I let this rose wilt into dust or stone?
Or will age and time blossom into a wine?
I'm trapped in fear of a tomb or hope for Rhone.

In life, you die burdened by crosses and time.
Hopefully Christened by shivers of passion.
In death, you bleed, made dressed as if you were fine.

A devil at the Gates to earn temptation...
In love, you find the truest damnation.

A Word of You

Morning blue eyes of grey
One more day to pursue
Dark lips of tonight pressed
to tomorrow to gain.

A glance without delay
A stop of knees we knew
A breath of yours and mine
I could never abstain.

Speak with lips and dissect
Unspoken to others
A mind to preserve all
And not again do feign

I'll sit still in this sway
And breathe a word of you.

Humor Me
pt. 5

Loser

He sat there, on his sticker-covered computer. He hasn't touched it in about five minutes. The screen is dark, and the keyboard no longer lights up. His left hand has been hovering over the base of his laptop, and his right hand is holding a coffee mug. He's leaned as far back as he can, with his right foot propped up on the chair in front of him.

He's been staring into the crowd the whole time. Glancing at each person's individual movements, and faces, and actions, and lovers. He smiles occasionally.   When he does, he starts typing, but then he deletes what he just wrote. Then his actions repeat. He can't commit.

He takes a sip of his coffee. By the angle he lifts it, it's almost empty. He continues to hold it regardless. His head is slightly bobbing back and forth. He's listening to music. Hip-hop. He's been here for two hours. For a moment he looks concerned. He feels in his pockets but only finds his keys. He sets them on the table and stares.

He starts typing again. This time it's more sudden. He pulls out his headphones and puts them into his bag. Closes his laptop, and repeats. He stands up and drapes his bag over his shoulder. Grabs his keys, and walks away, slowly.

Blue Ink

He's here every day. He has no name. He has no agenda. He has only time and the time to spend. He orders a 16oz coffee and sits in the same seat. He brings his black notebook and writes in blue ink

My Bakers Morning

The alarm goes off at 3 o'clock every morning. She wakes up too early, so I try to make it easier on her. I roll out of bed and start the coffee maker, I fire up the stove and make a simple breakfast. Eggs, kale, and granola. In the living room, we have a space heater; I turn it on to warm up the spot by the coffee table she likes to sit draped under a blanket while she drinks her coffee and eats her breakfast.

I go to wake her up. She usually goes into the bathroom to wash her face to help her feel more awake. While she's in there I move her breakfast and coffee into the living room onto the coffee table. She walks into the living room and sits on the floor in this spot. I'm usually lying on the couch behind her by this point. She puts a blanket over me and I drift off.

I wake up to her telling me that she's ready and she hands me a coffee in a thermos I put my shoes on before grabbing my keys. We drive on these dark neighborhood streets that are only lit up by porch lights. We don't talk much. I'm not a morning person. After a short drive, we reach the bakery she works at, and we kiss each other goodbye before she walks out of the car. I wait until I see her lock the front door of the shop before I drive off.

I make my way back home and go back to sleep for another couple of hours before I get up and start my day.

Mixtape

Come On Eileen, Dexys Midnight Runners

Trapped by a Thing Called Love, Denise LaSalle

A Sunday Kind of Love, Etta James

Bed Peace, Jhené Aiko, Childish Gambino

Tadow, Masego, FKJ

Something About Us, Daft Punk

Is it Any Wonder?, Durand Jones & the Indications

Fade into You, Mazzy Star

Leather and Lace *(with Don Henley)*, Stevie Nicks

Crimson & Clover, Tommy James & the Shondells

Lapsang Lunar Lovers

Single Serving:
2oz Hendricks
2oz Semi-Dry Riesling
.75oz Solerno
.5oz Fresh Orange Juice
.5oz Caravan Spice Simple Syrup with Brown Sugar
1oz Lapsang Souchong & Rosemary Hot Tea

Scaled for 10 Servings:
14oz Hendricks Gin 12oz Semi-Dry Riesling
6.5oz Lapsang Souchong & Rosemary Hot Tea
5oz Solerno Blood Orange Liqueur
3.5oz Fresh Orange Juice
3.5oz Caravan Spice Brown Sugar Simple Syrup

Serve Hot

This cocktail won me a free trip to Alaska.

Another Round?

"There's nothing in here!" I imagine that's what he's thinking every time he raises his glass to signal the bartender. He hasn't said anything. Hasn't even made eye contact. It's crowded in here, this guy has no chance of getting another drink unless he grows breasts. And he definitely doesn't have a chance of getting the attention of the woman he's been staring at.

He'll go home thirsty.

Laurel

Who am I to idolize dead poets?
And compare my voice to the Renaissance?
Abusing words for my gain like a ponce.
Etching these phrases out loud in public.
I scribble the truth to remain stoic.
The hypocrisy within is ensconced.
I am not Petrarch in term or in nonce.
Nonetheless, his words have raised at lowest.
A broken heart is not self-inflicted.
Vocation is permeable to love.
Death, while bitter, is not the end's quarrel.
So salt your wounds with hearts unpredicted
To align your path against stars above
And love for always like the bay laurel.

———

I gave up.
Then I found you.
Then you told me to fuck off.
So I downloaded Tinder.
...

I miss you.

Postcard

I'm sitting in the northernmost part of mainland Scotland. There are mountains behind me that appear unless. Valleys of lochs and rivers between every mountain. I'm outside right now sitting on a bench near a cliff that drops into the rushing North Sea. The lighthouse is spinning in the distance. The sky is so dark, I'm wishing for the Northern Lights, but the stars piercing through the grey clouds will have to suffice.

I've been wandering this ancient world looking for perspective. I've seen structures that are ageless, I've drank at pubs and taverns older than the US. I've stood near lakes and gardens that poets and wizards once called home. I've been looking for something to fill this missing part of me. Thinking maybe something truly magical could happen here. And while I've learned so much about myself and about how I need to stay humbled and grateful -- the thing I haven't quite found is the way you make me feel. I've been missing you. I've been thinking of you. I've not stopped loving you.

But I can't see the moon tonight.

www.ingramcontent.com/pod-product-compliance
Lightning Source LLC
Chambersburg PA
CBHW051222120626
46547CB00013B/1470